Wanderlust
WINING!

A Wine Country Activities Guide and
Travel Companion

Washington State

STEFANI JACKENTHAL

PRICE WORLD
PUBLISHING

Wanderlust Wining! A Wine Country Activities Guide and Travel Companion
Washington State
Copyright © 2011 by Stefani Jackenthal

Published by Price World Publishing, LLC
1300 W. Belmont Ave, Suite 20G
Chicago, IL 60657

First Edition, 2012
ISBN: 9781619840072

Printed in the United States of America
10 9 8 7 6 5 4 3 2 1

~ In memory of my Mom ~

To my Mother, Father, Cathy,
brothers Ron & Michael
and my superstar nephew
and niece Sam & Skylar!

Thank you for all of your love and support.

❦ Contents

Intro..7

Washington State 11

Fit and Sip Tips! 41

Fun Facts & FYI!... 51

❦ Intro

For years, I've been trying to convince my editors that active outdoors enthusiasts also have a great thirst for the fruit of the vine and love travel that blends the two. After all, what could be better than playing in beautiful lush rolling landscape and then drinking wine from grapes grown on the same fabulous fertile land?

As a long time adventure journalist and endurance racer, competing in road cycling, triathlon and Ironman, adventure racing, ultra-running and most recently surfski racing, my competitions and assignments have taken me to diverse locales around the globe. Many destinations have been surrounded by leafy vineyards and winery tasting rooms, just begging me to visit. What's a girl to do? Go with the flow, of course.

The thing is, I knew I wasn't alone in my quest for fun, endorphin-spiking activities followed by local, wine-sipping explorations. I was sure there were others like me who loved to start the day cycling winding back country roads, paddling sparkling waterways or hiking through fragrant forests and meadows blanketed with pastel wildflowers— and then spend afternoons connecting with regional tasting rooms for swirling, sniffing and sipping pleasure. Perhaps, tossing out a blanket in a grassy picnic area of one of the many wineries for an al fresco lunch overlooking trestled vines.

Adventure, wine and food naturally go together like, say, a triathlon or a three-course meal. As far as I'm concerned, wine is a food group. It's artistically crafted from fruit that grows in the ground and a treat on any dinner—or lunch—table.

Creating wine takes dedicated teamwork. First, grapes are lovingly planted and nurtured by savvy, skilled farmers, with a little luck from

Mother Nature. Grape farmers primp, prune and ultimately harvest the precious fruit while praying in sorts for a great growing season. From there, winemakers take over, blending their science and creativity in an inspired choreography of steps that transforms juicy fruit into the dynamically diverse wines we love so much.

Wanderlust Wining blends my two passions: outdoor activities and wine. In addition to being a journalist, I run a NYC-based wine events company called NTS Wine Tasting, LLC, crafting wine dinners, tastings and educational events, often featuring New World wines from across America.

The USA is the world's fourth-largest wine producing country, behind leaders France, Italy and Spain, and has been making wine for more than three centuries. Since North Dakota joined the mix in 2002, when Point of View Winery became the state's first federally bonded winery, each of the fifty U.S. states produces its own wine. While most states do not distribute beyond their regional or state border, most do ship and have fun tasting rooms to visit and sample local crafting.

I have meticulously peeked and poked into every nook and cranny of the selected wine tasting areas covered, chatting up locals for their insider scoops on the best places to play, sip and eat. As well as asking some wine-loving Olympic and professional athletes to share their favorite places in wine country to be sporty and then swirl, sniff and sip. I have created this book as a fun, playful, flavorful and informative insider's guide to exploring common and uncommon wineries in the area.

As if hanging out with a friend who lives locally, you will be taken on a journey through domestic wine countries, discovering how to create savory, action-packed wine tasting trips that kick off days with fun, local outdoor activities and follow up with palate-pleasing wines, food and assorted miscellaneous "cool things to do." I have given special attention to organic, sustainable and biodynamic vineyards, restaurants and lodging.

This book's fast-paced, easy-to-understand style offers easy to swallow wine information and historic facts about the area's wine specialties and unique geographic offerings, such as the best road or mountain bike rides, trails to traverse and rivers to paddle, as well as favorite farm-to-table restaurants and wine cave and vineyard tours. Learn where to go, who to contact and be privy to what "only the locals know" about amusing things to do such as Vino and Vinyasa, horseback riding wine tasting tours, learning to make cheese, attending outdoor concerts on winery estates or savoring a sustainable wine dinner.

Wanderlust Wining is a one stop read to crafting the ultimate fun, delicious wine-filled, active vacation.

Cheers to never-ending adventure and wine exploration!

Washington State

Washington State

Yakima Valley - Silver Lake Winery - Photo Courtesy of Yakima Valley Visitors & Convention Bureau

The second-largest wine producer in the USA, Washington State is behind California and a step ahead of Oregon. Still, while California has nearly half a million acres of vineyards, Washington has a mere 40,000. But, as they say, size doesn't always matter. With over 700 wineries as of 2010, up from 163 in 2000 and a mere 19 wineries back in 1981, Washington's fledging wine country is growing like teenage boy with hopes of an NBA contract.

Running north to south, the mammoth Cascade Mountain Range is a natural dividing line between eastern and western Washington, each with distinct climates. While the hilly western side encompassing Puget Sound waterways and islands is often cool and wet, the lush, eastern side enjoys a more moderate climate. In the east, where nearly 98 percent of Washington's wine grapes are grown in the Columbia Valley, it covers over one-third of the state and is the granddaddy AVA.

Unlike the capital city, Seattle, which has a steady supply of dank, rainy days (and is the western regional home to the Puget Sound AVA, which can receive upwards of forty-eight inches annually), Washington's eastern wine country gets just six inches of rain annually. Unlike California, Washington gets frosty winters, which allow vines go dormant and store nutrients until spring.

Meanwhile, the wild waterways attract paddlers, rafters and fly-fishermen and women from around the world. The region includes the Columbia, Yakima and

Snake Rivers, as well as a series of canals and wells, all of which supply wine growers ample water to meticulously control irrigation in this arid valley.

Boasting a multiplicity of microclimates from high deserts to rolling hillsides, the eastern side of the state gets over 300 days of sunshine with about 17 or more hours of sun-smooching. So, fruit here gets nearly two more hours of daily sunshine than California's grapes get in the summer months, plus cool nights allow grapes to retain bright acidity; overall cooler weather creates more "hang time," meaning that grapes are picked later in Washington than in California. So they have extra time to develop sugars and fruit flavors.

The fruit love-fest and unhurried picking pace pays big dividends, resulting in grapes that pack intense juicy flavors with bright acidity, resulting in dynamic wines with deep layers of fruit, texture and character. More than 30 wine grape varieties are produced here, nearly an even ratio of white to red: 52 percent white to 48 percent red. There's a varietal to put a smile on everyone's sipping lips.

Cabernet Sauvignon is the admiral of Washington State' wine fleet, packed with brambly dark berry and pungent plummy fruit with complex flavors and textures that unmask over time. Like an unsure teenage boy around a girl he likes, a young Cabernet Sauvignon kisses with subtlety and restraint, yet you sense the powerful potential that will develop with age. With maturity, the wine's confident core takes over with robust ripe raspberry, blackcurrant, dark chocolate-covered cherries with herbaceous, minty undertones.

Quickly gaining popularity through the state is its splendidly spicy Syrah, first planted in the Yakima Valley in 1986. This up-and-comer deep dark Rhône varietal is a wonderful partner in crime at the supper table with its concentrated blackcurrant, blackberry and mocha flavors that give way to hints of leather and loads of generous spice lasting through its luscious, long finish. Merlot, the most widely harvested red here, fills the glass with bright cherry aromas that lead to its cherry-red plum full body with discreet tannins.

Cabernet Franc, once mostly used as a blending grape can be found making solo appearances that pour with lovely dark blueberry, roasty-toasty coffee flavors, while the German grape, Lemberger, grows nicely in Washington, one of the rare places other than Germany where this diverse red variety thrives.

In the white world, expect to see a lot of Chardonnay, the state's most widely grown white. Some wineries are crafting this adaptable grape two ways, oaked and *au naturel*. While the un-wooded version can be reminiscent of biting into a bright, crisp Fuji apple, the Chardonnays aged in oak develop a golden hue and rich, creamy body and those receiving malolactic fermentation are loaded with caramel and buttered popcorn aromas and flavors. Not to be overlooked is the saucy Semillon, showing melon and fig in its youth and developing honey-nut nuances with age, whereas, the alluring Rieslings entice sippers with a fragrant floral nose and can run the gamut of off-dry to late harvest.

Get Dirty!

The expansive bucolic valley, shadowed by the Cascades, is dotted with picturesque evergreen trees, crimson fields and shimmering golden hillsides. Sporting scores of twisting back country trails frequented by hikers and bikers (and snowshoers in cold months), the craggy towering Cascades and Blue Mountains have glistening mountain lakes, streams and mighty waterways, like the Snake and Columbia Rivers, cutting through their etched ancient rock mass. The endless kayaking and rafting on the open river promises thrills and spills to splash happy folks. The trail's the limit for equestrians, hikers and mountain bikers, who can choose from countless trailheads leading to a network of trails cutting through old-growth forests, mountain meadows, mountain lakes and the myriad streams favored by anglers, especially for fly fishing.

In the canyons, bald eagles, especially in winter, can often be eye-spied, as can a variety of birds including over 21 species of raptors. On the water and in the woods, keep a look out for slick river otters, quick coyotes, cougars and deer, even bears. In the winter, two feeding stations near Naches let you view elk and bighorn sheep hanging out in their natural habitat.

While pedaling along open two-lane country roads can't be beat. With abundant out-of-the-saddle climbs up to *buena vistas* and speedy descents past fragrant orchards and clusters of vines lined up like soldiers at attention, interspersed with green and golden fertile farmland, it's a rush to the senses. The quad-pumping mountain biking on single tracks through twisty parks and wilderness trails can't be beat.

Rich in mountainous terrain, there is also world class rock climbing and plenty of snowboarding, skiing and cross-county skiing in the winter months. Then there is Mount Rainer, about two hours away, which is stockpiled with moss-carpeted, old-growth forest trails, gushing waterfalls, pastel wildflowers in high country meadows and, of course, its glacier peaks that attract mountaineers worldwide.

Malolactic Fermentation

Malolatic fermentation is part of the winemaking process for most red and a handful of white wines, especially Chardonnay. It is a secondary fermentation that converts aggressive, tart malic acid, like that found in a puckery apple, into softer lactic acid, which is common in cheeses and yogurt. Malo (as it is commonly called) fermentation aids in articulating the buttered popcorn aromas and flavors in Chardonnay and gives red wines a round, full mouth feel.

Planting Roots!

The first Washington wine grapes were planted at Fort Vancouver in 1825 by Hudson's Bay Company, now Canada's largest diversified general merchandise retailer with over 600 retail locations. There are records of Hybrid varieties in nurseries in the Puget Sound region in 1854 and grapevines planted in Walla Walla Valley in 1860.

Walla Walla - L'Ecole No 41 tasting room - Photo Credit: Walla Walla Tourism

With the influx of Italian and German immigrant in the mid- to late 1800s, by the turn of the century, there were wine grapes growing across much of the state, especially in Yakima and Columbia Valleys. The first annual Columbia River Valley Grape Carnival took place in Kennewick in 1910 and, four years later, notable vineyards, such as those belonging to W.B. Bridgman of Sunnyside, blossomed in the Yakima Valley. The fledging Washington wine industry was on the move.

But, as quick as a lightning strike, Prohibition hit in 1920 and was the ultimate kill-buzz. While the commercial wine industry ran dry, wine DIYers (that's "do-it-your selfers") honed their blending skills at home. With the end of Prohibition, the first bonded Northwest winery was established on Puget Sound's Stretch Island and by 1938 there were 42 accounted for wineries across the state.

On the heels of Prohibition, most Washington State wines were sticky, sweet sippers that "paired nicely with the state's sweet Vidalia onions." Not surprisingly, the commercial distribution options were limited.

In the mid-1960s, Washington's first commercial winery took root, with plantings that ultimately became today's Columbia Winery and Chateau Ste. Michelle Vineyards. As

Leon D. Adams wrote in "The Wines of America," originally published in 1973, "the Washington state recovery is one of the greatest human stories in the wine industry." Today, Washington State is the second-largest wine producer in America.

Wine to me!

Planted on fertile rolling hills, the vineyards in eastern Washington are bordered by Palouse on the east, the Okanogan Highlands to the north and by the Columbia River and Oregon's Blue Mountains on the south. It's Mother Nature's quintessential viticulture venture vacation spot.

There are five major viticulture appellations, which are defined specific geographic regions. The Columbia Valley, the biggest AVA, has three sub-appellations within its territory, Yakima Valley, Red Mountain, and Walla Walla Valley, while, in the western region, Puget Sound is the only officially acknowledged grape growing area.

The Yakima Valley appellation encompasses the Red Mountain AVA, the Rattlesnake Hills AVA and the Snipes Mountain AVA, and the Yakima Valley AVA's own boundaries lie completely within the much larger Columbia Valley appellation, as do the Wahluke Slope and Horse Heaven Hills. In 1983, the Yakima Valley appellation was determined as distinct from the larger Columbia Valley appellation that surrounds it, and it was authorized as an official American Viticultural Area (AVA/appellation). The three east-to-west geologic folds in the earth's crust, running east from the City of Yakima, the Ahtanum Ridge, the Rattlesnake Hills and

the Horse Heaven Hills, were the primary land masses associated with distinguishing the boundaries of this river valley carved by the Yakima River.

There are scores of boutique wineries with tasting rooms open to the public peppering the eastern region, while others require an appointment. Many are family-owned, whose owners and staff are eager to pour you some of their creamy Chardonnay, bright, crisp Riesling, and round of robust reds, including Cabernet Sauvignon, Merlot and spicy, earthy Syrah. Winery-hopping here promises an adventure around every bucolic twist and turn as each wine area and the wineries within have their own personality and charm. Some tastings are complimentary, while others charge a small fee, typically applied to bottle purchase.

Throughout the state, there are wine tastings and festivals held year round. In April, the Washington Wine Commission traditionally kicks off the spring and summer tourist season with a wine and food tasting in Seattle. Check out event calendar details on all the wine fun. www.washingtonwine.org.

Columbia Valley AVA

The Columbia Valley AVA is Washington's largest wine region with over 11 million acres, the region encompasses 18,000 square miles from the Okanogan wilderness up to Oregon, with the Columbia River acting as a natural boundary to the south, and continues east along the Snake River to Idaho. The Snake, Walla Walla, Yakima and Columbia Rivers are popular for whitewater rafting and kayaking in their big water, while there is coveted wind-

Walla Walla - Hot Air Baloon - Photo Credit: Walla Wall Tourism

surfing, kiteboarding and SUP in the less severe areas.

The Columbia Valley region on the west and north have infinite hiking, biking and horseback riding possibilities though the fragrant evergreen forests. Dotted and dashed with wildflowers and flowing streams, two of the highlights are the historical Lewis and Clark and The Oregon Trails.

Sporting a continental, high desert climate, grapes ripen slowly and evenly during hot days that are followed by cool nights that can drop as much as 25 to 40 degrees, which allows natural acids to be retain. Add to the recipe, an average of six to eight inches of rain falls annually, and the result is ideal conditions for producing Chardonnay, Semillon, Riesling, Merlot, Syrah and Cabernet Sauvignon.

The vast Columbia region contains six sub-appellations, including the Yakima Valley (an independent AVA), Walla Walla, Red Mountain and Horse Heaven Hills.

Yakima Valley AVA

Nestled in south central Washington, about a two to three hours' drive from Seattle, Spokane or Portland, the Yakima Valley AVA was established as a distinct AVA from the surrounding vast Columbia Valley in 1983. The state's oldest and largest appellation, it produces nearly one-third of Washington's grapes. Cozied up to the flanks of the foothills of the Cascade Mountains, which creates its western border, there are three sub-appellations; Red Mountain, Rattlesnake Hills and Snipes Mountain, the new kid on the block with just one winery.

The Valley offers as many wine touring options as there are grapes varietals growing in its vineyards planted in its lush rolling hillsides. There are numerous tasting rooms plunked down in historic downtown Yakima, such as Gilbert Cellar, known for their tasty tapas and live music, while big, bold red wine lovers flock to Kana Winery. Out of town, there are scores of tasting rooms peppering the two-lane country roads bounded by shaggy vine, orchards and farms in and around Zillah and Wapato, in Prosser, pouring wines with familiar names such as Hogue Cellars, Chinook and Kestrel Vinters, and fledgling Benton City within the Red Mountains.

Get Dirty!

With over 300 days of sunshine and a cornucopia of outdoor opportunities, Yakima Valley is a one stop shop to sip, stay and play. There are pristine trail systems cutting through naturally defined mountain ranges, a sundry of stunning landscapes including jagged hillsides, pillowy meadows, dynamic waterways and striking sheer basalt cliffs all waiting to be accessed.

Yakima Valley boasts a network of trails that are perfect for a grab bag of adventures ranging from hiking and biking, trekking and rock climbing, horseback riding, mountaineering, snowshoeing, skiing and beyond, not to mention the wild waterways slicing between basalt cliffs along the canyons formed by centuries-old volcanic upheavals. Attracting bald eagles, notably in the winter, over twenty species of raptors, a variety of glo-

rious birds often soar overhead, while a menagerie of wildlife, such as river otters, coyotes, cougars, bears and deer scamper through the forest. In the winter, two feeding stations near Naches are fantastic viewing spots for elk and bighorn sheep in their natural habitat.

Some popular spots include Tieton River Canyon, Yakima River Canyon, Cowiche Canyon and Snow Mountain Ranch. With four trailheads across 1800 acres, Cowiche Canyon and Snow Mountain Ranch sports fourteen miles smack in the middle of Yakima, which makes it the local go-to for fantastic for hiking, cross-country skiing and snowshoeing. About twenty miles west of the downtown of Yakima, the 20,000 acres of wilderness in Tieton River Canyon are quilted with miles of heel-worn trails past old growth trees and clusters of wildflowers and world class rapids. While the 27- mile Yakima River Canyon is laced with sheer basalt cliff rising over 2000 feet about the flowing river. Cycling along Yakima Canyon Road (Washington 821), offers delightful eye candy with its multi-colored rock ridges cutting along the narrow gorge and plethora of birds and wildlife.

Not to be forgotten are nearby White and Chinook Passes, both gushing with waterfalls and alpine lakes along the eastern Washington portion of the Pacific Crest Trail. The trails within their lush wilderness and shrub-steppe landscape offer top-notch mountain biking, hiking and horseback riding. There is even a 200-foot-long trail on the Boulder Cave Trail within Chinook Pass, and breathtaking Boulder Cave Falls.

Cycling along the Yakima Valley's long stretches of two-lane rolling hills on country roads is good for the heart and soul, and a pretty nifty way to shape your booty. Mother's Nature puts forth her best eye candy to melt away the miles of pedaling past fruit orchards, over scenic ridgelines, through jagged canyons and alongside vineyards with emerald green vines growing shoulder-high. There are great rides in which to break a sweat before settling into an afternoon of sipping or riding to and from vineyards in a multi-tasking sipping exploration. Keep an eye out for nasty Goat Heads, a low-to-the ground weed with piercing, sharp thorns that will puncture a bicycle tire faster than you can say "Cheers!" Local riders tend to use thorn-proof tires, plastic thorn shields; regardless, bring extra tubes and patches.

"The Yakima Valley is a wealth of fun bike rides and there are quite a few riders around too," says David Lowe, who runs Wineglass Cellars in Zillah with his wife and son. "Zillah is in the 'Lower Valley' from Yakima and on the other side (north and west) there are lots of rides that are quite lovely, too." He recommends riding the one from a shopping center along the old Naches Highway to Naches, crossing the river and looping back to the shopping center. "Its fun, beautiful and quite well used by bicyclists living in Yakima," he notes, adding that the county police have put up "do not block traffic" signs for the cyclists as there is a time trial course set up there. Lowe has created a 60-mile cycling loop, "Lowe 60-miler," starting at his winery that can be broken into a great 35-miler. [[see sidebar for Lowe 60-miler]]

For some out-of-the saddle climb, head west of Yakima and choose from a plethora of routes in Eschback Park, Naches Heights or Lake Wenas. For a chilled morning cruise, take a spin through the Yakima River Canyon, which is the route for the annual "Your Canyon for a Day" Bike Tour, held in May. The Yakima Greenway, a 10-mile paved path through 3600 acres of fertile flora and farmland parallels the Yakima River, connecting three parks, two lakes and rivers with a handful of river access landings. The path is popular with cyclists, runners and in-line skaters. Bike rentals are available at an assortment of bike shops specking the valleys.

Of course, sipping and spinning past vineyards, orchards and farmstands selling fresh cherries is always a healthy and eco-friendly way to pedal your way through a palate-pleasing day. If you are traveling in September, you may want to jump into the Wine Country Trek, a bike tour of wine country from Yakima to Prosser for the Great Prosser Balloon Rally.

There is also terrific ride through the heart of wine country, along Yakima's Konowac Pass on what's locally called the "Wine and Fruit Challenge." Snaking across the verdant farmland peppered with vineyards and fruit trees, this 31-mile easy-to-moderate loop with a few long climbs crisscrosses past seven wineries and/or tasting rooms. Those seeking a big, butt-busting day in the saddle can take on the longer, 87-mile version of this ride. Contact the Zillah Chamber of Commerce for details, www.zillahchamber.com.

For a schmoozy rail-to-trail ride, check out the 14-mile Lower Yakima Valley Pathway from Sunnyside to Prosser. The paved route is mostly flat, making it popular with runners and skaters. About two miles

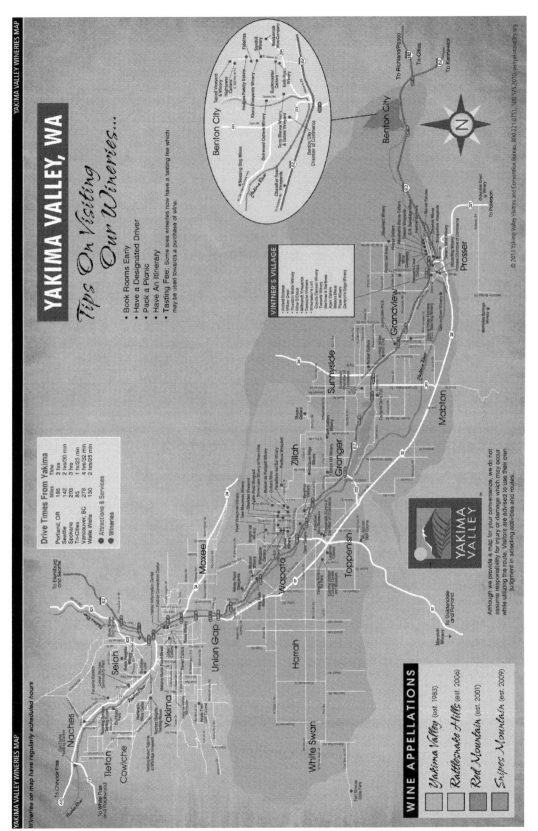

Yakima Valley Wine Map - Photo Credit: ©2011 Yakima Valley Visitors & Convention Bureau

Zilah - Wineglass Cellars Tasting Room - Photo Credit: Wineglass Cellars

from the Sunnyside trailhead, the Lower Valley County Park has restrooms, water and shady areas for picnicking.

Some of the area's finest mountain biking is found on the Cowiche Canyons Upland Trail, part of the 80-acre Cowiche Canyon Natural Preserve. There are scores of twisting, undulating, single and double-track trails with some substantial climbs to awesome overlooks that are frequented by mountain bikers and hikers. There is also a web of rock climbing routes suited for newbies to super Spideys. After your day of play, you may want to hop on the half-mile long side trail (located just west of the Uplands Trail junction, next to the footbridge) that connects to The Tasting Room Washington (formerly Wilridge Winery) on Ehler Road in Naches Heights.

Many of the locals head to Bumping Lake and Rimrock Lake to cool off on hot summer days with a dip in chilly mountain lakes. The numerous trailheads bypassing the lakes and zigzagging through the Yakima Valley are ideal for trail running, hiking or feeling the cool mountain air blowing through your hair while galloping on horseback.

There are terrific traditional and sport climbing options for newbies to seasoned Spideys in the Tieton River area, which is accessible from White Pass (Highway 12). The volcanic rock, shaped by lava flows, which created Adesite columns, a type of basalt unique to this region, is a novel treat. With nearly 400 routes, many of them nearly vertical and some sporting jagged overhangs, it's a sweet climbing spot to spend the day exploring. Other nearby destinations include Frenchman Coulee, Vantage and Banks Lake, in nearby Grant County. A few hours in the car will take you to the flanks of Mount Rainier or Mount Adams for major mountaineering up to glacial peaks.

In recent years, Yakima River has become a hotbed for trout stream and fly fishing, while its big, gushing spring water from the snowmelt off the mountains brings a smile to adrenaline junkies and whitewater paddling technicians alike.

In the summer months, much of the beastly wild whitewater is calmed and although there are still fun, run-able sections, the Yakima and Snake Rivers attract folks seeking mellow float trips through the cliff-rimmed canyons. Outfitter Rill Adventures on Old Thorp Highway leads guided rafting trips and provides a shuttle service. They also do some very cool full moon float trips in the summer months.

When the mercury drops, snow bunnies scamper to snow sport destinations areas smattering the state and a short drive from wine country, such as snowboarding-friendly Mount Baker, near Bellingham, which gets up to 645 inches of snow seasonally, more snow than any other ski slope on the continent!

 East Everett on Highway 2, Stevens Pass is another popular destination for those seeking slopes of varying degrees of difficulty, quick lifts and heart-pumping mogul hills. While in Wenatchee, the Mission Ridge ski area has spectacular panoramic views of the Cascade Range. As well, the White Pass Ski Area has excellent Alpine and Nordic facilities.

Greg Barton, two-time Olympic gold medalist and president of Epic Kayaks.

"When visiting Yakima in the winter, I Nordic ski at White Pass. One unique winery is Blackwood Canyon. While most of the others have expanded into large, upscale, relatively sterile tasting rooms, Blackwood is a dive with authentic dust-covered barrels teetering on top of each other. Mike, the head winemaster, is either a genius, crazy or both."

Wine to Me!

Sharing the same latitude with premier wine-producing regions of France, Yakima Valley has over 82 wineries and three sub-appellations, Red Mountain with 12 wineries; Rattlesnake Hills, established in 2006 with 17 wineries and the most recent "official" sub-appellation, established in early 2009, is Snipes Mountain, near Sunnyside, with just one winery and counting. Their distinct volcanic soils, microclimates, and topography are the secret ingredients to produce more than 30 different types of wine, but around here red wine, especially Cabernet Sauvignon, Syrah, Merlot and Cabernet Franc, are the leaders of the pack.

Some of the area's top winemakers may sound familiar, such as Covey Run, Hogue and Côte Bonneville, receiving kudos in the press and tradeshows. However, most of the boutique wineries with tasting rooms are family-owned and the owners and winemaker are often on hand to chat about their wines.

Zilah - Wineglass Cellars Tasting Room
Photo Credit: Wineglass Cellars

reational" vineyard. Boasting 80 acres of hiking and biking trails, with great rock climbing routes, not surprisingly, the property of course has vineyards, orchards and stunning sageland bluffs. Set up in a 1900s farmhouse, there are over 20 wines from four wineries, to sample. To get there by bike or on foot from Cowiche Canyons Upland Trail, in Cowiche Canyon Conservancy, look for a half-mile-long side trail located just west of the Uplands Trail junction (next to the footbridge) that connects the to The Tasting Room, at 25o Ehler Road. Give them a call at 509-966-0686 if you get lost.

With the bulk of its wineries and vineyard on or near Interstate 82, winery-hopping here is a breeze. Tasting rooms are conveniently clustered together making them ideal cycling and sipping destinations, while driving is cool, too. Pack up your picnic baskets or backpacks and have fun savoring the Washington wine-soaked days as you swirl, sniff and sip through Yakima Valley's wine country, in downtown Prosser, with 25 tasting rooms pouring wines with familiar names such as Hogue Cellars and Kestrel Vintners.

To the southeast is Rattlesnake Hill Wine Trail running from Wapato to Zillah, home to many family-run wineries with lovely picnic areas, so it's a good idea to swing by a deli or market in town and pack up your picnic basket with goodies. Getting kudos on that trail for its big reds is Portteus Vineyards & Winery, which was called "one of America's great producers of Cabernet Sauvignon," by *Wine Enthusiast* magazine, while the folks at Wineglass Cellars will uncork local bicycle route knowledge as you sip and schmooze. Just ask owner

With the bulk of its wineries and vineyard on or near Interstate 82, winery-hopping here is a breeze. Tasting rooms are conveniently clustered together making them ideal cycling and sipping destinations, while driving is cool, too. Pack up your picnic baskets or backpacks and have fun savoring the Washington wine-soaked days as you swirl, sniff and sip through Yakima Valley's wine country.

There's a nice selection of tasting rooms in downtown Yakima, like Gilbert Cellars, known for their organic wines and live music on some nights of the week. To the northwest of town, on Naches Heights, you won't want to miss The Tasting Room Yakima at Wilridge Vineyards, on Ehler Road. Part of a cooperative of four wineries, it's said to be Washington's first "rec-

David Lowe about the Lowe 60-miler.

Further southeast, Prosser has 25 tasting rooms pouring some well-known brands and at the very eastern edge of Yakima Valley, Benton City (part of Red Mountain AVA) is getting lots of buzz for their big and beefy, yet well-balanced Cabernet Sauvignons and spicy Syrahs.

There are wine tastings and festivals held throughout the state year round and the Washington Wine Commission sparks the spring-summer tourist season with a wine and food tasting in Seattle, held in April. Check out event calendar details on the Wine Commission's website, www.washingtonwine.org.

Downtown Yakima & Naches Heights

There are quite a few fun and friendly tasting rooms in Downtown Yakima and on its outskirts, including Gilbert Cellars, Kana Winery, Treveri Cellars, sparkling wine specialists. To the northwest, Naches Heights is home to The Tasting Room Yakima at Wildridge Winery, a cooperative of four wineries (Harlequin, Naches Heights Vineyard and Wildridge Winery) set up in a 1900s farmhouse. Nestled within the Cowiche Canyon Nature Preserve, it's truly an outdoorsy oenophile's dream come true. The winemaker at Wildrige, Paul Beveridge, is also a talented ceramic artist who showcases his work and that of other artists at the onsite art gallery.

Wineries

Gilbert Cellars 5 North Front Street, Suite 100, Yakima, WA 98901 * 509- **249-9049 * www.gilbertcellars.com** Open daily; hours vary. With live music, this contemporary tasting room pours certified organic estate wines that pair perfectly with their tapas and cheese selections.

Kana Winery 10 South 2nd Street Yakima, WA 98901 * 509-453-6611 * www. kanawinery.com Open daily. Their big, bold reds are as fiery (not hot, but powerful) as their name, Kana, a native word for the spirit or the fire within mountain, referring to the perceived supernatural power of volcanic activity. They are crafting old vine blends using Lemberger, Tempranillo and Syrah.

Treveri Cellars 225 S. 2nd Avenue, Yakima, WA 98902 * 509-248-0200 * www. trevericellars.com Open daily (on weekends in winter). Sparkling wine specialists using assorted varietals.

The Tasting Room Yakima (Wilridge Vineyard) 250 Ehler Road, Yakima, WA 98908 * 509.966.0686 *www.wilridgewinery.com Open Thurs-Mon. This certified organic and biodynamic vineyard and tasting room near Yakima is housed in a 1900s-era farmhouse next to the Cowiche Canyon Nature Preserve and is, perhaps, Washington's inaugural recreational vineyard. The bucolic property includes 80 acres of hiking and biking trails, rock climbing routes, vineyards, a tasting room and art gallery, and a gorgeous picnic area. Winemaker Paul Beveridge is serious about his work and play. Located about five minutes from Yakima, off Highway 12 and Naches Heights Road, Wilridge Vineyard is part of one of Washington's first cooperative tasting rooms representing four boutique WA wineries:

Harlequin Wine Cellars, Mountain Dome Winery, Naches Heights Vineyards and Wilridge Winery and Vineyard. With over 20 wines available by the glass or bottle, there is something for everyone. It's a perfect prescription for recovery after a hardcore play session!

Rattlesnake Wine Trail & Lower Yakima Valley

Forming the northern border of the Central Yakima Valley, the Rattlesnake Hill wine trail starts about four miles southeast of Yakima and west of Prosser, off Interstate 82. Often referred to as the 'green' tour of the Yakima Valley, the Rattlesnake Hills that include the towns of Zillah and Wapato, was established in 2006 and sits in the low rolling hills and prime farmland with lovely vineyard views and picnic areas. Wineries on the trail are found between exits 44 (on the west) and exit 63 (on the east) along the Highway. Portteus, on Highland Drive, is a must go for red wine lovers. Called "One of America's Great Cabernet Producers" by *Wine Enthusiast* magazine, they take Cabernets seriously, but not themselves. Their tasting room is warm and welcoming and the wines … well, you decide.

If you're planning to visit the bulk of Rattlesnake Hills wineries, you may want to purchase a ten-dollar "Passport" at the Yakima Valley Visitors Center from any of the wineries. Show your passport at any of the seventeen Rattlesnake Hill wineries and receive a special treat like discount on wine or free reserve tastings. If you really lush it up and hit ten wineries, you will be invited to attend the annual Rattlesnake Hill Picnic in late summer.

The wine trail is pouring with characters and wildly wonderful wines. Be sure to ask David Lowe at Wineglass Cellars for cycling suggestions — he's gear head to the max (that's a huge compliment!) Sip along with the working winemaker tending to barrel and tanks at Horizon's Edge, and the folks at Maison de Padgett Winery promise wines "with a twist" and apparently, they throw a good party, too.

Every Sunday morning there are guided 60-minute winery and 90-minute vineyard tours of Rattlesnake Hills led by winegrowers or winemakers. Reservations are required: 509-965-4521.

Wineries

Wineglass Cellars 260 N Bonair Road, Zillah, WA * 509-829-3011 * www.wineglasscellars.com As enthusiastic about cycling as he is about winemaking, David Lowe will pour you a taste of his ripe, rich Capizimo red blend while he spills the beans about awesome rides around Yakima Valley. He runs the winery with his wife Linda and son Jeff and this family affair is all about flavorful wine and good fun. Lowe has developed a 60-miler for Wine Trail pedalers that combines long stretches of wending country roads and gear-clicking rolling hills through the vine-rich Valley. It's sure to work up a big thirst that can be quenched with some other house specialties, including unoaked Chardonnay, Cabernet Franc and Syrah.

Portteus Winery 5201 Highland Drive, Zillah, WA 98953 * 509.829.6970 * www.portteus.com Open daily. "One

LOWE'S 60-MILER

LOWE'S 60-MILER – Bicycle Ride is courtesy of David Lowe, owner of Wineglass Cellars, Zillah, WA * www.wineglasscellars.com

Starting Line: Take interstate 82 East through Yakima. Take Exit 40, turn right and park at the park-and-ride just on the right.
 Go right out of the park and ride.

0.3 miles - turn right across the Parker Bridge

0.3 miles - you have to turn left onto North Track. This road has some really bad potholes so be careful. It's boringly straight and flat.

4.5 miles Stop sign in the middle of Wapato go straight through staying on North Track.

11.1 miles Welcome to Toppenish. At the end of North Track (there is a fire station on the left) go across Buena Way onto Asotin. At Les Schwab Tire Center go left onto Lincoln Avenue.

1.0 miles At the end of Lincoln Avenue turn right on to "L" street.

0.7 miles At stop sign turn left and on to South Track. This is a good road, flat and fast. Have you warmed up yet? The hills are coming; you can see them out there on the left.

3.8 miles At the stop sign go left. There is no road sign but it's Hwy 223 North. Go over the RR crossing and the Yakima River.

2.5 miles Turn right onto Emerald Road. This is a hard right. Warm up is over. We'll start with some easy hills first.

1.3 miles Turn Left onto Cherry Hill. This is only a short way to the top but a nice leg burner. At the top is the old Stewart Winery. If you look hard enough you can probably find some water faucet to refill bottles if you need to.

0.6 miles Going down Cherry Hill you'll find Gap Road. Turn right onto it.

2.0 miles. At this stop sign you're at Luther. If you want, Luther is only a mile and one of the steepest climbs around. Great downhill once you turn around at the Transfer Station. But when you're finished with Luther and back at the stop sign turn left and go under the freeway. You come to Yakima Valley Highway and straight across Luther turns into Dekker. If you want to avoid the hills, turn left onto Yakima Valley Highway and follow it all the way back to your car.

5.6 miles At the top of Dekker, this is getting fun, eh? Turn left onto Houghton.

2.0 miles Nice view at the peak of Houghton of Mt Adams and the valley. At the stop sign turn right onto Beam. And then left again onto Houghton.

3.0 miles Nice rollers you've just gone through. Now you have to go left onto Highland

2.4 miles Turn right onto Roza (on the left you'll see Maison de Padgett).

1.0 miles At the top of Roza you have to go left onto Gilbert. The winery on the left is Sheridan . . . good stuff.Vi

2.9 miles At the end of Gilbert turn right onto Knight Hill

1.1 miles At the "T" of Lombard Loop Road turn left and stay on this road as it winds it's way up the hill.

1.9 miles After a nasty little leg burner and then a short downhill turn right onto Nightingale Road.

3.7 miles At stop sign you are now on the top of Konnowac Pass and it's all downhill now.

2.2 miles At the Konnowac Pass "Y" turn left . I don't know what this road is named because the sign is down.

0.7 miles Turn right onto Laframboise Road

0.5 miles Turn left onto Gamache Road. This road sign was down when I mapped this out too, but it's the first left.

1.9 miles Gamache Road turns into Thorp road. Stay on this and it will take you back to your car.

3.1 miles Thorp Road becomes Yakima Valley Highway and just on the other side of the freeway is where you parked your car.

of America's Great Cabernet Producers," according to *Wine Enthusiast* magazine. Producing only 100 percent Estate-bottled wines, their award-winning Cabernet Sauvignon overflows with chocolatey, brambly blackberry. They are made crushing the Syrah, Zinfandel and Cabernet Franc.

Bonair Winery 500 South Bonair Road, Zillah, WA * 509-829-6027 * www. bonairwine.com Open daily. This quarter-century-old, family-run winery uses estate-grown grapes to produce their award-winning Chardonnay, Cabernet Franc and Cabernet Sauvignon. They serve tasty tapas Friday through Sunday in the summer.

Maison de Padgett Winery 2231 Roza Drive, Zillah, WA 98953 * 509-829-6412 *509.829.6401 * www.maisonde-padgettwinery.com Open Thursday–Monday. A boutique vineyard "specializing in good conversation and quality wine," their quaint tasting room has a stunning panoramic view of the bucolic surroundings. Don't miss the European Gardens or shady patio for a picnic.

Horizon's Edge Winery 4530 East Zillah Drive, Zillah, WA 98953 * 509-829-6401 * www.horizonsedgewinery.com Open Thursday–Monday, seasonally. The tasting room is set up inside their "working winery," to give visitors of taste of the elbow grease and ingenuity that is poured into their small batch winecrafting.

Benton City

This small but mighty wine region in the Red Mountains, on the eastern end of the Yakima town, has gained a big reputation for their reds. In fact, most of their 700 or so acres of vineyards are dedicated to red wine grapes. Topping the list of "people's choice award" varietals are Cabernet Sauvignon, Merlot, Syrah and Cabernet Franc. Much of Red Mountain is covered by Worden silt loam-type soil, which retains minimum moisture and contains nominal organic material. While the seemingly toxic combination makes the grapes struggle for survival, it actually channels the vine's energy straight to the source — the berries. Ah, another lesson in what doesn't kill you makes you stronger. The surroundings, while beautiful, are a bit barren, but the winemaking is full of life at its more than 15 wineries.

Wineries

Kiona Vineyards and Winery 44612 N Sunset Road,Benton City WA 99320 * **509-588-6716 *www.kionawine.com** Open daily. The snazzy tasting room has vaulted wood ceilings, granite tasting bars and Terrazzo-style concrete floors with a bird's-eye view of the 10,000-square-foot underground barrel cellar. The covered patio overlooks the vineyard and the gallery features local artists.

Terra Blanca Winery and Estate Vineyard 34715 N Demoss Road, Benton City, WA 99320 * 509-588-6082 * www. terrablanca.com Among Red Mountain's premier red wine producers, specializing in Merlot, Cabernet Sauvignon, Syrah , and Chardonnay for the white wine lovers in the crowd. They are certified Salmon-Safe, meaning their wine grape growing practices have been audited and meet standards that protect biodiversity, water quality and fish and wildlife habitats, particularly native salmon populations.

Fidelitas Winery 51810 N Sunset Road * Benton City WA 99320 * 509.588.3469 * www.fidelitaswines.com Open daily. A boutique winery that is "faithful" to Cabernet Sauvignon and "loyal" to Bordeaux, that produces small lot, handcrafted expressive reds.

High Tower Cellars 9418 E. 583 PR NE, Benton City, WA *509-588-2867 * www.hightowercellars.com Open Friday–Sunday. Crafting complex Cabernet Sauvignon, Merlot, Syrah and more from grapes grown in the Horse Heaven Hills, Red Mountain and Walla Walla Valley appellations.

Prosser

With more than 30 tasting rooms and some big girls, like Hogue Cellars, Kestrel Cellars and Chinook, Prosser is definitely an urban wine tasting experience. Peppered between fast food joints and filling stations, just off the highway it's no stroll in the park. Still, the wine's terrific and if you are coming from downtown, you will need to pass through en route to Benton City. If in need of a lunch spot, Willow Crest Winery has a bistro and patio just off its tasting room.

On Friday nights, from April to October, Kestrel, Snoqualmie, Desert Wind, Hogue Cellars, Heaven's Cave, Alexandria Nicole Cellars, Cowan and Mercer have coordinated a "Sip and Stroll." The wineries stay open until 7 p.m., many offering bites and flights, if your punch card is filled by the end of the evening you will be eligible for the big prize drawing. Like you need more encouragement to drink.

Snoqualmie Vineyards 660 Frontier Road, Prosser, WA 99350 * 509.786.2104 * www.snoqualmie.com Open daily. Their "Naked" organic series is made with certified organically grown grapes in a certified organic facility, while the "Nearly Naked" wines are just as flavorful but not quite getting the big "O."

Hogue Cellars 2800 Lee Road, Prosser WA, 99350 800-565-9779 509-786-6108 www.hoguecellars.com Open daily. Pouring their Hogue, Genesis and Reserve series.

Kestrel Winery Kestrel Vintners 2890 Lee Road, Prosser, WA 99350 *509-786-2675 * 888-343-2675 *http://kestrel-wines.com Open daily. Serving flights and bites, and "Simple Super," every third Friday of the month. Picnic area.

Alexandria Nicole Cellars 2880 Lee Rd, Suite D , Prosser, WA * 509-786-3497 * www.alexandrianicolecellars.com Open daily. Producing small lots, handcrafted wine from their Destiny Ridge Estate Vineyard, overlooking the Columbia River. They serve meat and cheese plates to nibble alongside their selection of wines.

Willow Crest Winery 590 Merlot Drive , Prosser, WA 99350 *509-786-7999 *www.willowcrestwinery.com Their bistro will whip you up lunch to enjoy on the patio with a glass of Chardonnay or Mourvedre. The Syrah Port is a nice way to cap off the visit.

Wildlife Viewing
Wildlife viewing of elk in Yakima Valley

Winter is a wonderful time to visit the Oak Creek Elk Feeding Station, on Highway 12, about twenty miles west of downtown Yakima. When grazing ends in higher elevations, in the winter months, up to two thousand Rocky Mountain elk mosey down to the feeding area for their daily ration of hay at about 1:30pm, when an early supper is served. The mass of majestic mammoth mammals in motion is simply a breathtaking sight that gets sparked by the sound of the hay truck motors, which starts the action. The Oak Creek Winter Feeding program, begun in 1945, is a terrific opportunity to get up close and hopefully, not too personal with these wonderful wild beasts. Nearby, at the junction of Highways 12 and 410, there is often a small herd of California big horn sheep, so keep your eyes peeled. Oak Creek Wildlife Area 16601 Highway 12 Naches, WA 98937 * 509.653.2390 * www.wdfw.wa.gov

The Dirty Facts!

Cycling

Prosser Balloon Festival * 800-221-0751 * www.prosserballoonrally.org A fully-supported cycling event through Washington wine country, held annually in September, stopping at over fifty Yakima Valley wineries in route to the Prosser Balloon Festival, in Prosser, WA.

Columbia Valley Cycling Society: www.columbiavalleycyclingsociety.org Runs weekly group rides of varying levels and distances. Calendar is posted on website as are some fun local mountain biking trail maps.

Washington's Department of Transportation (maps) * www.wsdot.wa.gov/Bike

The Bicycle Alliance of Washington * (events, clubs & resources) * www.wsdot.wa.gov/Bike

Hiking

Washington Trail Association: www.wta.org

The Cascadians: www.cascadians.org Offering group trips along the Valley's numerous trail systems.

Rafting Outfitters

Columbia Rafting 250-427-3266 *877-777-RAFT. www.columbiarafting.com A one stop rafting (and more) company in the Columbia Valley. Guiding whitewater canyon trips in the Columbia Valley and horseback riding, hiking and mountain biking in the Rocky and Purcell Mountains.

Osprey Rafting Co. Leavenworth, WA 98826 * 888-548-6850 * ospreyrafting.com

Yakima Rill Adventures, Inc. 10471 N. Thorp Highway, Thorp, WA 98946 *

888-281-1561 * 509-964-2520 * rillsonline.com

Kayaking Outfitters

Columbia Kayak Adventures 509-947-5901 * www.columbiakayakadventures.com Leading guided tours on inland lakes and Upper Columbia, the Snake and Yakima Rivers. Rentals available too.

Washington Kayak Club www.WashingtonKayakClub.org

Washington Water Trails www.WWTA.org

Skiing

Washington Ski Touring Club, Seattle, WA, 206-784-8741 * wstc.org

Rock Climbing

Yakima Climbing Club 509-965-9262. Hosts informal monthly meetings, hooks up climbing partners and shares local "best area climbing" information.

Miscellaneous

Zillah Chamber of Commerce for details 509-829-5055, www.zillahchamber.com).

Visit Rainier: Ashford, WA 98304 * 877-270-7155 * 360-748-4514 * VisitRainier.com

Downhill and Cross-Country Skiing

White Pass Scenic Byway Packwood, WA 98361 *111 S. 18th Street * Yakima, WA 98901 * 360-494-2323 * whitepassbyway.com

The White Pass Ski Area has excellent Alpine and Nordic facilities and even offers a number of summer activities at the White Pass Village Inn, including bird watching, fishing and swimming. Alpine skiing and snowboard enthusiasts will revel in the 350 inches of annual snowfall, the five ski lifts and the 1,500-foot vertical drop.

Yakima Greenway Foundation 509-453-8280 * yakimagreenway.org

Yakima Area Arboretum 1401 Arboretum Drive, Yakima, WA 98901 * 509-248-7337 * ahtrees.org

Wine Tours Run by Local Experts

Vineyard Tours - 509-965-4521 Advanced reservations required. Sunday Mornings, starting at 9am, 90-minute guided tour of the vineyards of the Rattlesnake Hills led by winegrower or winemaker. Fee $10 per person.

Winery Tours - 509-965-4521 Advanced reservations required. Sunday Mornings, starting at 9am, 60-minute guided tour of one of the wineries in Rattlesnake Hills led by qualified wine expert. Fee $10 per person.

Feed Me!

Greystone Restaurant 5 North Front Street, Yakima, WA 98901 * 509.248.9801 www.greystonedining.

com Casual fine dining in the Historic District with a *Wine Spectator* award-winning wine list. Pick from the menu at the bistro bar or sit down for supper and enjoy regional and classic entrées. Reservations suggested.

Santiago's Gourmet Mexican Restaurant 111 E. Yakima Avenue, WA 509-453-1644 www.santiagos.org Did someone say fish tacos? Yum! A local favorite serving fun, flavorful fare such as fajita salads, Chipotle Steak Tortas and their house specialty "Taco Santiago's," best enjoyed alongside a margarita sidewalk café.

Picazo 7Seventeen Wine Bar & Restaurant, 717 6th Street, Prosser, WA 99350 * 509-786-1116 * www.picazo717.com Closed Sundays. A Spanish-inspired wine bar and restaurant showcasing local fare and wines, offering wine and food pairings.

Café Mélange 7 North Front Street, Yakima, WA *509-453-0571 * http://cafemelangeyakima.com. This cute wooden paneled café in downtown is a true "farm-to-table" delight as is their in-house pasta made from organic semolina flour. Their cozy homemade seasonal desserts are the perfect way to wrap up a fun day.

Bella an Italian Deli, 502 9th Street, Benton City, WA 99320 *509-588-3354 A quaint cozy cottage turned deli serving modern Italian classic soups, salads and panini.

Essencia Bakery 4. N 3rd Street, Yakima, WA * 509-575-5570 * www.essenciaartisanbakery.com Warm crusty bread and handcrafted croissants, sticky buns and cheesecakes are all fantastic choices enjoyed alongside an eye-opening espresso or latté and a lovely lunch spot too.

The Yakima Valley Museum Soda Fountain 2105 Tieton Drive, Yakima, WA 98902 * 509-248-0747 * www.yakimavalleymuseum.org/soda An old-fashioned working exhibit of a late 1930s soda fountain with friendly soda jerks and all, serving ice cream sodas, sundaes and milkshakes.

Darigold Dairyfair 400 Alexander Road, Sunnyside, WA 98944 * 509.837.4321 * www.darigold.com Open daily. Take a fun tour of a cheese-making factory and discover the secret to making more than 174 million pounds of cheese a year.

Snoozing!

Apple Country Bed & Breakfast 4561 Old Naches Hwy Yakima/Naches, WA 98937

509-965-0344 * 877 -788-9963 * www. applecountryinn.com

Cavanaugh's at Yakima Center 607 East Yakima Avenue, Yakima, WA 98901

509-248-5900 * 800-325-4000

Orchard Inn Bed & Breakfast 1207 Pecks Canyon Road Yakima, WA 98908 * 509-966-1283 * 866-966-1283 * www. orchardinnbb.com

Wine Country Camping

Yakima Sportsman State Park 904 University Parkway, Yakima, WA 98901 * 509-575-2774 888-226-7688 * yakima.sportsman@parks.wa.gov

Walla Walla

About an hour's flight from Seattle, Walla Walla is the "the town so nice they named it twice," according to the Chamber of Commerce. Known for robust, rich, ripe Cabernet Sauvignon, Merlot and Syrah, Walla Walla is also renowned for their Walla Walla Sweet Onions that some swear are candy-sweet; in 2007, it was designated the official vegetable of Washington State. The onion is such a power player that Canoe Ridge Vineyards holds an annual onion dinner where local chefs create wine-friendly onion dishes to pair with Canoe Ridge Merlot and other varietals.

Located in southeast Washington, Walla Walla is east of the Cascade Mountains on the flanks of the Blue Mountains and expands across the Columbia River into the northeastern pocket of Oregon. It is also a common meeting point of Washington, Oregon and Idaho. Established in 1984 and expanded in 2001, there are over 70 wineries here that source most of their grapes from the 50 or so vineyards planted in deep, well-draining silt soil, known as "loess." Some of their grapes are grown across the Columbia River in Oregon.

Similar to its Mama AVA, Columbia Valley, Walla Walla, meaning "many waters," in Cayuse Indians' native tongue, enjoys hot, long, sunny days and cool mountain

Walla Walla Onions
Onion Power

The Walla Walla Sweet Onion was introduced to Washington State over a century ago, when Peter Pieri, a French soldier, brought the sweet onion seed to America. However, the mild variety of onion does not originate from France. Pieri discovered it while he was in Corsica, an island off the west coast of Italy.

evenings to nurture grapes with deep expressive flavors and bright natural acidity. The western Cascade Mountain border restrains rainfall to less than 13 inches annually, resulting in an expansive fertile valley quilted with golden hillsides and emerald green evergreen trees that offers outdoors enthusiasts a lush wilderness playground.

Get Dirty!

This charming wine country town packs a big punch of outdoor opportunities. Hill-phobic runners and cyclists will love the relatively level Walla Walla Valley terrain and the network of paved trails running through the Valley from Rooks Park, east of town, to the College Place city limits, near Fort Walla Walla Park, that make a dandy morning workout. Those looking for longer, more challenging routes can pick up a Walla Walla cycling map at bike shops and many of downtown locations or request one at www.wallawalla.org. Also, check in with Walla Walla Valley Cycling www.wwvalleycycling.com and the Wheatland Wheelers for more cycling information. The map lists some fun rides. such as the 30-miler called "Mill Creek," which is a gradual steady climb for about

15 miles to Camp Kiwanis, followed by a zippy downhill ride home.

For a historic two-wheel tour, check out the "Whitman Mission" ride (between 16 and 24 miles, depending on route) passing the Whitman Mission National Historic Site and then there's a 50-miler, called "Harris Park," with some gradual climbs to the Harris Park Campground, whereas, the knobby tire crowd can hit the trails in the Blue Mountains, an hour's drive from Walla Walla, which has two ski resorts, Spout Spring and Ski Bluewood, frequented by locals in the wintertime.

Exploring wineries on two wheels is a breeze and folks at Bicycle Barn or Allegro Cyclery will gladly rent you a bike for the day or week. Many of the wineries are grouped within pedaling distance of each other and there is a plethora of scenic road rides on country roads, past golden dancing wheat fields painted across lush, forest green, rolling hillsides dotted with tall Evergreens zigzagging past colorful farm stands selling gooseberries, asparagus and spinach in the spring and blackberries, raspberries, cherries, pears and of course, onions in the summer months. Be sure to load up on picnic goodies like artisan cheeses, cured meats, fresh bread and even pasta to go at Cugini Import Italian Foods. Many of the wineries have lovely picnic spots. If you'd rather skip the schlepping, schedule a lunch stop at CreekTown Café and fill up on Dagwood-sized sandwiches, crunchy salads and juicy burgers made from locally raised beef.

For a full day of wilderness play, Walla Walla's Whitman College Outdoor program, not only leads hiking, kayaking, rafting, climbing and ski trips for non-students and students, but they offer gear equipment, too. It's a good deal for newbies visiting the area in search of local outdoor experiences and a chance to get into the mountains, and offers sparkling Snake and Columbia rivers, which are favorites for paddling, rafting and fly-fishing.

Fickle fitness folks who like options can head over to the 200- acre-plus Fort Walla Walla Sports Complex, Walla Walla's largest park with a 70-acre wildlife preserve with undulating hiking trails and gurgling streams that are an ideal picnic setting. The mammoth athletic Mecca also has volleyball courts, Dreamland Skate Park, BMX Track and eighteen-hole Frisbee golf course, and picnic tables. At night, the amphitheater is home base for entertainment.

Planting Roots!

Grape growing in this area dates back to the 1850s when Italian immigrants began planting vines and making wine, half a century after Lewis and Clark trekked through the area in 1805 and again in 1806. The first post-Prohibition winery, Blue Mountain Vineyards, was launched in 1950 by the Pesciallo Family, who grew Italian varietals including Black Prince. Despite high hopes, their winery never took root and closed. Walla Walla's modern wine industry came to attention in the 1970s when two Army Reserve buddies, Gary Figgins and Rick Small, pioneered the land. Figgins, then an amateur winemaker who was inspired by a wine trip to the California vineyards started Leonetti Cellar in 1977, so-called in honor of his maternal grandparents, who were Italian immigrants. Leonetti Cabernet Sauvignons have gained cult status and the small productions keep massageingthe mystique. By 1990, five wineries made up the Walla Walla AVA, and now there are over 35 and counting.

Wine to me!

Using earth-friendly practices, Walla Walla viticulturists and oenologists minimize their impact on Mother Nature by producing wine through sustainable methods, using the natural advantages of their environment to enrich the wine's bold flavors and rich layers. Cultivated in the foothills of the Blue Mountains in rural Washington, Walla Walla's fiercely flavorful grapes are grown in what is considered one of the most diverse appellations in the country.

There are five main wine touring and tasting areas through Walla Walla's wine country, including the downtown area, south, west and east of town and the Airport area. In addition, there are plenty of charming inns, market-fresh restaurants and art galleries. Similar to the wineries, many of the twenty or so farms and dairies, such as Ross's Spring Creek Farm, Blue Mountain Lavender Farm and Cavalli's Onion Acres Farm, are open for visits by appointment and some offer "U-pick" your own produce.

Downtown Walla Walla

Super-convenient for those snoozing in town who can leave the car key in the room to stretch legs and winery-hop amongst the more than 20 tasting rooms sprinkled through the charming brick road town. One of the standouts is Sleight of Hand Cellars, launched in 2007 and named one of the "The Next Cult Wineries" in Washington State by *Seattle Magazine* in 2009. Visiting their tasting room is sort of like stepping into a Harry Potter-style winery – if he had one – where they are crafting fun flavorful wines such as the Magician, a double blend of 60 percent Gewurztraminer and 40 percent Riesling, an aromatic bright white showing ripe peaches and Anjou pears. Some of their reds include the Spellbinder Red Blend and Levitation Syrah made from 100 percent Syrah sourced from vineyards in Walla Walla and Yakima Valleys and oak-aged to delight discriminating palates with roasty dark purple fruit flavors and dense mouth-filling tannins from its inky-black, bodacious body.

And there's DaMa Winery, where chicks rule and winemaker Dawn Kammer and Mary Tuuri Derby (as in Da' Ma') are crafting vibrant Viognier, Cowgirl Cabernet Sauvignon and Syrah they note as "a subtle, sexy wine. There's just the right amount of body and mysterious dark fruit to know you are dealing with a wine that wants to be noticed. She's a little spicy but finishes with an everlasting smokiness." Their artsy labels are just as alluring.

Wineries

DaMa 45 East Main Street, Walla Walla, WA 45 East Main Street * 509-520-9687 * www.damawines.com A fashion-forward winery making "approachable and affordable wines," named for the owners and winemakers Dawn Kammer and Mary Tuuri Derby, that also means "lady" in Spanish.

Sleight of Hand Cellars, 16 North 2nd Avenue, Walla Walla, WA * 509-525-3661 * www. SofHcellars.com. Open Thur–Sun 11–5, April thru December 5th and by appointment. Crafting wines like the Magician, Levitation Syrah and Spellbinder Red Blend.

Forgeron Cellars 33 W Birch Street Walla Walla, WA * 509-522-9463 * www.forgeroncellars.com Open daily. Meaning "blacksmith" in French, Forgeron winery and tasting room was formerly a blacksmith shop, but is now getting kudos for its Cabernet Sauvignon, Zinfandel and late-harvest Semillon.

Canoe Ridge Vineyard 1102 West Cherry Street, Walla Walla, WA * 509-527-0885 * www.canoeridgevineyard.com Open daily. Focused on estate grown Cabernet Sauvignon and Merlot. Hosts an annual onion dinner where local chefs create oenophile-friendly onion dishes to surgically pair with Canoe Ridge wines.

South of Walla Walla

Just a few minutes drive, or a bit more by bike, this wine trail near the Oregon border has over 20 wineries amongst verdant vineyards. White wine lovers should not miss Rulo Winery's Chardonnays. Their barrel-fermented Birch Creek is every bit as rich and creamy as those favoring that style demand, while their un-wooded Chard unmasks the fruit, which radiates through citrusy,d peachy flavors. Northstar Winery and neighboring Pepper Bridge Winery (and Seven Hills) are red wine specialists getting sumo ratings from reviews and visitors alike. Just say "Northstar" in these parts and dark, velvety Merlot will follow. Getting high marks for their selection of seductively smooth, chocolate-cherry Merlots, it's a full-on party in a glass. Pepper Bridge and Seven Hills practice sustainable viticulture for fashioning fabulous Merlot, Cabernet Sauvignon, and Bordeaux-style Reserve. Flying under the radar but not to be overlooked is Tertulia Cellars, which is doing magical things with its LeCollines Syrah, Sobra blend and Carmenère, old world-style wine with deep dried dark fruit and splash of pepper and spice that gives way to soft tannins and a long finish.

Wineries

Northstar Winery 1736 J.B. George Road-Walla Walla, WA * 866-486-7828 * www.northstarwinery.com Open Daily. The stone contemporary winery and tasting room has a panoramic view of the breathtaking Blue Mountains. Their lovely patio with tables is perfect for picnicking with a glass of their award-winning, silky Merlot.

Pepper Bridge and Seven Hills, 1704 J.B. George Rd.Walla Walla, WA 99362 * 509-525-6502 * www.pepperbridge.com. Open daily. Producing Merlot, Cabernet Sauvignon, Malbec, Tempranillo and Bordeaux-style wines using sustainable methods.

Tertulia Cellars 1564 Whiteley Road-Walla Walla, WA * 509-525-5700 * www.tertuliacellars.com Open Thursdays–Saturdays, 11–6, Sundays 11–5 and by appointment. Known for Syrah, Sobra, Carmenère and Grenache.

Isenhower Cellars 3471 Pranger Road, Walla Walla, WA * 509-526-7896 * www.isenhowercellars.com. Open Thursdays–Sundays or by appointment. They have a second tasting room in Woodinville, WA.

Beresan Winery 1956 J.B. George Rd Walla Walla , WA *509-522-2395 * www.beresanwines.com Open Fridays and Saturdays. Crafting Cabernet Sauvignon, Merlot and tongue-tapping, spicy, chocolate-berry Cabernet Franc.

West of Walla Walla

Somewhat near the Tri-Cities and heading toward Yakima Valley wine country, when heading west, young lads and ladies, expect a bit of remote rambling landscape, unlike the other areas. But it's worth the trip, especially a stop at L'Ecole No 41 winery, set up in a 1915 schoolhouse, turned winery and tasting room, complete with chalkboard, ladder-adorned bookshelves and school bell. The winery's name is derived from the French word meaning "the school" that was once located in district 41. Not only will their handcrafted, barrel-aged Semillon, Chardonnay, Merlot, Syrah and Cabernet Sauvignon certainly get high marks for palatial pleasure, but their sustainable wine production practices

East of Walla Walla & Walla Walla Airport Wineries
See website www.wanderlustwining.com to learn about wineries east of Walla Wall and Walla Walla Airport region.

sponsorship of a regional bicycling racing team get an A+ all around.

Wineries

L'Ecole No 41 Winery 41 Lowden School Road, Lowden, WA 509-525-0940 * www.lecole.com * GPS: 118.581166W/46.056784N Open daily.

Woodward Canyon Winery 11920 W. Highway 12 in Lowden, WA * 509-525-4129 * www.woodwardcanyon.com Open daily. Their charming tasting room is set in a 1870s farmhouse where they pour Barbera, Chardonnay and an "artist" series of Cabernet Sauvignons.

Feed Me!

The CreekTown Cafe 1129 S. Second Avenue, Walla Walla, WA * 509-522-4777 * www.creektowncafe.com A terrific lunch spot for salad, sandwiches and burgers.

Grapefields 4 East Main Street, Walla Walla, WA * 509-522-3993 Nicole Bunker's wine shop posing as a bistro — or is it a bistro posing as a wine shop? You decide. Either way, it is the perfect place to pick through the shelves for a sipping partner to pair with her hearty fare.

Whitehouse-Crawford Restaurant 55 West Cherry Street, Walla Walla, WA 99362 * 509-525-2222 * www.whitehousecrawford.com Set up in an old mill, built in 1904, they feature local fare and Walla Walla wines.

Cugini Import Italian Foods 960 Wallula Avenue, Walla Walla, WA * 509-526-0809 * www.cuginiimportfoods.com

Walla Walla Valley Farmers Market: Saturday and Sundays, May 1–October 30th in downtown Walla Walla

Farms & Dairies

Ross's Spring Creek Farm 3782 Old Milton Highway, Walla Walla, WA * 509-525-7009 Pick your own sweet corn, tomatoes, apples, cantaloupes and more. Open daily in season.

Blue Mountain Lavender Farm 245 Short Road, Lowden, WA * 5059-529-3279 *www.bluemountainlavender.com Pick your own lavender flowers from 15 varieties or take a craft class. Open daily in season.

The Dirty Facts!

Bicycling

Walla Walla Valley Cycling * www.wwvalleycycling.com Cycling information about the area.

Wheatland Wheelers 509.301.2348 ***www.wheatlandwheelers.com Local cycling group.

Whitman College Outdoor Program * 509.527.5965 * www.whitman.edu/content/outdoor-program Offering organized group rides.

Bike Rentals

Bicycle Barn www.bicyclebarn.com

Allegro Cyclery www.allegrocyclery.com

Whiteman College Outdoor Program Rental Shop 345 Boyer Avenue, Walla Walla, WA * 509-527-5965 *www.whitman.edu Located at Reid Campus Center, OP organizes outdoor adventure trips including, hiking, paddling, climbing and skiing, and offers gear rental.

Skiing

Ski Bluewood- 509-382-4725 * www.bluewood.com. Beginner to expert terrain for skiers and snowboarders.

Spout Springs – 541-566-0320 *www.skispoutsprings.com. At Tollgate Mountain in northeast Oregon, offering downhill and cross-country trails.

Swimming

Joe Humbert Family Aquatic Center * 541-938-9166.

Dreamland Skatepark – www.skatewallawalla.org sporting halfpipes and more for tricked-out skateboarders

BMX Track

wallawallabmx.org a pro-style BMX Track at Fort Wall Walla Park

Snoozing!

Mill House Lodging and Events 504 N. First St. Dayton, WA 99328 509-382-2393 www.millhouselodging.com

The Marcus Whitman Hotel and Conference Center 6 West Rose Street, Walla Walla, WA 99362 * 866-826-9422 * www.marcuswhitmanhotel.com

The Maxwell House Bed and Breakfast 701 Boyer Avenue, Walla Walla, WA 99362 509-529-4283 www.themaxwellhouse.com

Wine Tours

Caveman Coach Limousine Services 710 May Ave, Walla Walla, WA *509-529-7170 Full day guided tours of Walla Walla wineries.

Blue Stocking Tours 6 West Rose Street, Walla Walla, WA * 509-522-4717 Customized wine and fly-fishing tours

Columbia Gorge & Puget Sound

See website www.wanderlustwining.com to learn about wineries and outdoor activities in Washington's Columbia Gorge and Puget Sound.

Sip and Fit Tips!

Wine Tasting Tips

Just like Mom used to say, "just taste it and spit it out if you don't like it." Nothing wrong with spitting in the wine worlds. Exploring wineries is the perfect time to sip and taste wines you ordinarily wouldn't order or buy. There are endless selections best under-stood and remembered by putting it across your palate. To optimize the experience, its nice to swirl the wine in the glass, take a couple of big sniffs, and then sip and savor it, rather than quickly gulping. If it sucks or your pacing yourself - or if you're the desig-nated driver, spit it in the spittoon, which you'll find somewhere on the tasting bar. Oh, and watch out for the backsplash.

When tasting wine:

- **Swirl** – Swish the wine around in the glass to mix it with oxygen, allowing the "bouquet" to release — the wine's fruit aromas.

- **Sniff** – Stick your nose into the glass — no, really, stick your nose in there to get a good whiff. Now, take two big sniffs as if you walked into Grandma's house while she's baking chocolate chip cookies. What do you smell? Is it fresh? Spicy? Fruity?

- **Sip** – Briefly hold wine on tongue and don't swallow yet. Instead, think back to grade school when you made kissy-faces at the girl or boy you liked or fish faces at your brother or sister. Besides feeling like an idiot, the goals is pull oxygen across the wine so the flavors (and aromas) can release and be detected. Think about the flavors and textures (thick or thin) from the be-ginning of the sip to the middle and after you have swallowed, the lingering flavor known as "the finish." How does it taste and feel immediately, in mid-dle and after swallowing. What you expected? Is it fruity? Earthy? Puckery? Spicy? Soft?

Fit Tips on the Road

by Amie Hoff, Fitness Consultant and Co-Founder of www.FitKit.com, creator of FitKitTRAV-EL, a portable lightweight selection of total-body workout tools with an exercise library for staying fit on the road.

Some adventures on your trip may be a workout in themselves, but add the fabulous wine drinking and epicurean delights and you'll want to be sure to make exercise a part of your daily itinerary.

If you plan ahead and pack a few lightweight workout tools, you won't lose your exercise momentum on the road. Follow these simple fitness tips to stay energized, sleep better and keep off the unwanted pounds that might creep up while you're off traipsing the country:

- Research local running or walking routes. Running and walking are great ways to explore the area and get in a little cardio. www.mapmyrun.com is a nice resource for many routes all over the world.

- Check your hotel for a workout room or ask if they have a partnership deal with local gyms.

Here are a few "on the road" exercises to make the wine taste all the better!

Exercises

Mountain Climber with a Twist

Works: Cardio, arms, core

Start: With hands on the ground, just under your shoulders and on your toes and back flat.

Movement: Keeping your elbows soft, draw one knee into the opposite armpit and back out, then bringing the other into the armpit without stopping between.

Tip: Keep your abs tight

"T" Push Up

Works: Chest, shoulders, abs

Start: On your toes and one hand placed a bit wider than shoulder width and in line with the chest, fingers facing forward. Other arm is raised in the air.

Movement: Bring the arm down and place it just wider than shoulder width. Bend the elbows to a 90-degree angle, lowering the chest towards the ground, keeping your back flat. Press through the chest and back up to starting position, raising the arm and twisting to the opposite side.

Tip: Keep abs tight to help with balance.

Side Lunge with Tap

Works: Hips, inner thigh, quads

Start: Stand with feet hip's width apart and hands at your sides.

Movement: Take a large step to the side with one foot, toes facing forward. Lean into traveling leg, bending at the hip and knee. Reach opposite arm over to touch the outside of the traveling foot. Push back up to starting position.

Tip: Try to keep your knee from traveling past your toes.

Glute Stretch

Movement: Lie on your back with left ankle over the right knee. Hold both hands behind the right knee and draw both legs to the chest.

Tip: Try to keep hips on the floor.

Running Tips

by Deena Kastor, New Mommy, Olympic bronze marathoner & American record holder in the marathon.

Running Form:

1. Run relaxed in body and mind.

2. Focus on softening your hands and face.

3. Run tall as if your head was being pulled up towards the heavens.

4. When running hills, emphasize sound biomechanics by driving knees and pumping arms.

General Tips:

1. Hydrate: During runs, drink 3 to 4 oz. of fluids every 15-20 minutes for any run over 60 minutes, and continuously drink water throughout the day.

2. Eat a good source of protein and carbohydrates within 30 minutes of finishing your workout to ensure recovery for your next run.

3. Run with a group, as running with others brings out the best in each of us.

4. Treat yourself well with massages, stretching, good nutrition and sound sleep. This not only improves your running, but will benefit your work and social life, too.

5. Choose a scenic route to invigorate your running routine, like wine country, which is a great place to explore.

6. Try to have at least 50 to 100 miles on your ASICS before race day, to ensure your shoes are well broken in.

Mountain Biking Tips

by Rebecca "Queen of Pain" Rusch, three-time 24-hour solo mountain bike world champion and two-time Leadville 100 winner and women's record holder.

1. Get a bike that is professionally fit to you. Just like your favorite jeans, bike fit is very personal and makes a huge difference in your comfort, enjoyment and skill progression.

2. Get off your butt and get comfortable moving your body around over your bike on easy terrain, then transition to the harder stuff. Unlike road cycling, mountain biking is a full-body, dynamic sport, requiring you to pedal while standing, sitting, tossing your bike side to side and moving your weight forward and back according to the terrain and obstacles.

3. Curb your enthusiasm. Going up and down curbs is a great, controlled way to practice getting over logs and rocks. Practice lifting the front wheel and moving your weight back, then moving it forward to get over the curb —practice with your weight back and you can even "hop" the bike off the curb. Repeat until you are ready for the trails and then practice technical trail sections over and over until you feel comfortable doing it.

4. Look where you want to go. This seems obvious, but it's common to stare at the scary obstacles and steer into them. Look just past it where you want your bike to go.

5. Speed is your friend. Getting over obstacles requires momentum. If you approach an obstacle too slowly, the wheels can get stuck upon contact with a rock or root, while speedy wheels stay in motion. With wheels rolling, you can often breeze right over the tough stuff.

6. Let the air out. Most riders have too much tire pressure, which can create less traction. In general, tires with tubes should run at about 30 pounds, while tubeless tires can go around 20 pounds. Find what works for you and check it every time you ride. Keep in mind that softer tire pressure equals bigger contact patch equals better traction equals better control and more fun.

Disclaimer

A word of caution: riding a bicycle is potentially dangerous, especially while sipping and spinning to tour tasting rooms on two wheels. It's a good idea to set up a wine tasting strategy to retaining sharp focus and balance on the bike. Adding "spitting" to the three S's (swirl, sniff, sip) is one suggestion. Have fun and be safe!

Fun Facts & FYI!

Fun Wine Facts!

- One barrel of wine equals about 20 cases, 240 bottles or nearly 1,200 glasses.

- Every bottle of wine contains just under three pounds of grapes, which means that, since you can get about five glasses of wine from a bottle, each glass contains a little over half a pound of grapes.

- A ton of grapes makes about 720 bottles of wine, or 60 cases.

- One vine can produces between four and six bottles of wine annually, equaling 20 to 30 glasses.

- There are typically between 15 and 45 clusters of grapes per vine.

- One acre of land can nurture between 900 and 1,300 vines.

- How do you say Gewürztraminer? Like this: "Ga-virtz-tra-meener" or just call it Gewürz for short, which is pronounced "Ga-virtz."

- In 2010 the U.S.A became the world's biggest wine-consuming nation, over-taking France. [[Source: according to the report from consultants Gomberg, Fredrikson & Associates.]]

FYI!

What are Tannins?

The grittiness and tartness from the residue of the grape skins, seeds and stems used in the winemaking process, which give wine structure, texture and aging potential. It is similar to the dry, gravelly, tart tongue sensation when slugging down that last sip of coffee or tea. In the latter case, the tannins come from the coffee bean or tea leaf residue.

While tannic wines can make great "food wines," too much tannin may be an indication that the wine needs more cellar time, as long as plenty of fruit is present. Over time, tannin mellows as a wine hits its height in complexity and enjoyment.

- **Too Much Tannin**: Common to young wines, can create a pucker effect, a harsh grittiness followed by an intense desire to brush one's teeth.

- **Too Little Tannin**: Often found in wines beyond their prime, the wine will taste and feel flat, lifeless, sour and thin.

- **Just the Right Amount of Tannin**: Wine will show with pleasing texture, ample fruit and lively complexity.

Tasting Wine with Food

First, sip the wine and swish it around your mouth. Notice the fruit flavors, which parts of your tongue detect the different flavors, and how it "feels" on your tongue. Then chomp into a piece of grilled meat, eggplant or mushroom. Sip again! Scrutinize how the wine reacts with the food. Does the wine taste different? If so, how? Is it more or less powerful? Did the flavor or texture of the wine change? Did the wine pick up qualities in the food or vice versa? Is there a lingering flavor in your mouth? These are terrific questions to ask yourself as you sip your way through a variety of varietals paired with fare.

Steel- versus Oak- (Barrel) Aged Wines

- **Steel-aged:** Wines processed and aged in big steel vats, such as a New Zealand Sauvignon Blanc, which preserves bright, crisp, snappy, fresh fruit flavors and aroma. Keep in mind that an acidic white wine that may taste puckery will tone down with appropriate food such as crunchy green, goat cheese or grilled chicken – while brightening the flavor of the food. Sipping an acidic white wine like a Sauvignon Blanc with say an oyster will act like squeezing lemon on the oyster an bolster its flavor.

- **Oak- (barrel) aged:** Wines aged in oak, for example, most California Chardonnay, resulting in toasty, buttered popcorn and/or caramel aromas and flavors.

Clink, Clink!

The tradition of clinking glasses can be traced to medieval times. Back in those days, it was common to kill your enemy by poisoning his food or drink and wine's tannins were ideal for masking poison. To prove his wine safe, the host would pour a bit of his guest's wine into his own glass and drink it first. But, if the guest trusted his host, he would simply clink goblets with him. Thus, this clink became a festive sound of trust and celebration.

Glossary

For a glossary of helpful terms, check out www.wanderlustwining.com

Made in the USA
Middletown, DE
01 August 2021

45194796R00033